LYME DISEASE

—Diseases and People—

LYME DISEASE

Scott Veggeberg

Enslow Publishers, Inc.

44 Fadem Road	PO Box 38
Box 699	Aldershot
Springfield, NJ 07081	Hants GU12 6BP
USA	UK

Library of Congress Cataloging-in-Publication Data

Veggeberg, Scott.
    Lyme disease / Scott Veggeberg.
        p. cm. —(Diseases and people)
    Includes bibliographical references and index.
    Summary: Explores the history of Lyme disease and discusses its symptoms, diagnosis,
prevention, and treatment.
    ISBN 0-7660-1052-X
    1. Lyme disease—Juvenile literature. [1. Lyme disease.]
    I. Title. II. Series.
RC155.5.V44 1998
616.9'2—dc21   97-34042
                                                          CIP
                                                          AC

Printed in the United States of America

10 9 8 7 6 5 4 3 2

Illustration Credits: Enslow Publishers, Inc., p. 33; Erik Johnson/Scandanivanian
Photography, p.18; MedImmune, Inc., pp. 82, 83; National Institutes of Health,
pp. 11, 20, 23, 37, 49, 65; New Jersey Governor's Office, p. 57; Scott Veggeberg,
pp. 28, 35, 42, 47, 63, 71, 72, 74.

Cover Illustration: National Institutes of Health

Contents

LYME DISEASE

What is it? An infection caused by spiral-shaped bacteria called *Borrelia burgdorferi*.

Who gets it? Almost anyone who spends time outdoors in places where deer ticks carry the *Borrelia burgdorferi* bacteria. Animals, including a pet dog or cat, can also be infected.

How do you get it? The bacteria that cause Lyme disease are carried inside the bodies of deer ticks (*Ixodes scapularis*). When a deer tick infected with the bacteria burrows its head into the skin of a person or an animal, the bacteria will slowly migrate from the tick's gut into its mouth, and then into the skin it has bitten.

What are the symptoms? The most common symptom, appearing in up to 60 to 80 percent of people infected, is a skin rash called erythema migrans (EM). The rash begins as a small red circle at the site of the tick bite. The red ring spreads outward and usually reaches six to twelve inches in diameter. Once it gets this large, the center of the rash usually clears up, and it begins to look like a bull's-eye. Other symptoms include fever and chills, headaches, fatigue, and joint and muscle pain.

How is it treated? In its earliest stages, Lyme disease can be easily treated with oral antibiotics. Usually amoxicillin (a form of penicillin) or doxycycline (a form of tetracycline) is taken for about twenty days. If Lyme disease is not detected right away or if it invades the nervous system, a person might have to take intravenous doses of more potent antibiotics.

How can it be prevented? Lyme disease is found in the coastal areas of the Northeast, in some parts of Wisconsin and Minnesota, and in the coastal areas of Oregon and California. People in these areas should take precautions against ticks. These precautions include tucking pants into socks, wearing long-sleeved shirts and light-colored clothing when walking in the woods, and applying insect repellents designed to ward off ticks. After spending time outdoors in an area where Lyme disease exists, people should check themselves carefully for ticks.

Three Lyme Disease Stories

enry, an eleven-year-old sixth grader, used to live in Brooklyn, just across the river from the skyscrapers of New York City. Although his parents enjoyed the museums, parks, and lively nightlife of the city, they thought a move to the suburbs would be the best way to escape the overcrowding, crime, and other woes of a big, gritty city. So they uprooted the family and settled in Pleasantville, a suburb about an hour's drive north. As its name suggests, Pleasantville is a pretty nice town, with no shortage of parks, nature preserves, and other wide-open spaces. Henry quickly shifted his roving from city sidewalks to forest trails, crashing his bike over stumps, roots, and rocks, instead of curbs and grates.[1]

Wide-open spaces may look nice, but they sometimes have their own set of dangers. They are home to foxes, opossums, and raccoons, all of which can be dangerous if they contract rabies. There are also deer, mice, and the occasional ticks that live off their blood—something his parents had not counted on.

One day Henry got up in the morning feeling strange. One whole side of his face felt numb, and he could not get his mouth or cheek to move properly. It felt the same as when he went to the dentist and had his mouth numbed by Novocain. When he showed his droopy face to his mother, who is a doctor, she was alarmed. To her medically trained eye, Henry had a condition called Bell's palsy. This condition occurs when the nerve running down the side of the face becomes paralyzed. She knew Bell's palsy is not the sort of thing you usually see in children. It shows up in people who have a viral infection, a head injury, or a tumor that has grown so large that it starts pressing on a nerve. Sometimes, however, Bell's palsy is seen in children who have been bitten by one of the tiniest creatures found in the woods—the deer tick.

The deer tick, which can be as small as the period at the end of this sentence, is not by itself a menace. It means no harm. All it wants out of you is a bit of your blood for nourishment. The trouble is that about 10 percent of these minuscule ticks carry even tinier passengers—bacteria called *Borrelia burgdorferi*. These bacteria are the troublemakers that actually cause Lyme disease.

Henry's mother could have drawn his blood and given him a test for Lyme disease, but the tests often come back negative when a person has been infected for only a few days. The test may even be negative when a person has been infected for

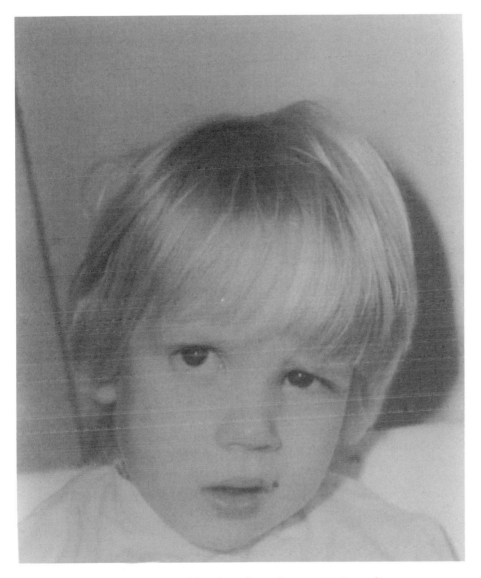

Bell's palsy is a kind of facial paralysis often seen in Lyme disease.

quite a while. As it turns out, the county they moved to, Westchester County, has one of the highest rates of Lyme disease in the entire country. About two thousand cases are reported every year.[2] Also, it was summer, which is the height of the Lyme disease season. Henry's mother decided to take no chances and immediately put him on antibiotics. Within a few days Henry's lopsided smile began to return to normal. A year later, he had no further symptoms of the disease.

Jason is ten years old and in fifth grade. People say he is a pretty terrific drummer, banging away on the bongos, the conga, and other African drums. When he is not pounding out a rhythm, he spends much of his spare time outdoors, exploring in the nearby woods or playing football. One day when Jason was six, his mother was running her hand through his hair and she discovered a bizarre rash. It was enormous, about twelve inches around, and completely covered by his hair. It probably would never have been seen if his mother had not accidentally found it. Jason says he remembers being incredibly tired most of the day. He was so tired that he wanted to sleep all the time. Whenever he sat down, he did not want to get up again.[3]

When his mother took him to the doctor, the rash was not easy to see, so the doctor decided to do a blood test. The test came back positive for Lyme disease. The doctor told Jason he was lucky. When a ring-shaped rash is found, it usually means the disease has been discovered early, when it is still easy to treat. His doctor prescribed antibiotic capsules, which Jason took three times a day. Within a couple of weeks, he felt fine.

Now Jason knows to wear light-colored clothing and check himself for ticks whenever he has been outdoors. By being careful, he has been able to avoid getting Lyme disease again.

Norm was a sixteen-year-old high school student when he met up with a tick, but he was not as lucky as Henry and Jason.[4] While Norm was living in Germany as an exchange student, his host family took him to the Czech Republic for a holiday camping trip. Norm never saw the tick that bit him, but after the trip he did notice a strange circular rash that kept increasing in size until it was as big as a half-dollar. He showed the rash to a German doctor, who thought it might have been from a tick bite but was not sure. He prescribed two weeks of antibiotics, and the rash went away. After Norm returned to the United States a few months later, though, he began to get headaches. They were mild at first, but puzzling because he never had them before. At first Norm thought the cause might be allergies. But when the headaches got much worse, and he started getting pain and swelling in his right knee, he decided to visit his family doctor.

At first the doctor was baffled. But after Norm told him about the rash in Germany, the doctor began to suspect that Norm had contracted Lyme disease. It was possible that the bacteria had not been completely killed by the antibiotics and had traveled into his brain and joints. When the tests came back negative for active Lyme disease, the doctor really did not know what to make of it. After reading more about the disease, the doctor told Norm that he had what is called post-Lyme disease syndrome (PLDS). Medical researchers are not in agreement on exactly what PLDS is. It might be that the bacteria are hiding in the cells of the body. Other medical researchers think that the symptoms are actually caused when the body's immune system has somehow been fooled into attacking its own body. This type of illness is called autoimmune disease.

Whatever the cause, Norm's symptoms were very real, forcing him to spend practically all of the next two years in bed with pain and fatigue. Although he feels better now and has finished high school, it is still not clear in his mind, or in the mind of his doctors, just what went wrong.

These are the two faces of Lyme disease. For the majority of people, like Henry and Jason, Lyme disease is simply an annoyance and not much worse than a bad case of the flu. In rare cases, however, it can turn into a long-term, strength-sapping disease. Fortunately, the National Institutes of Health (NIH) is now conducting a major research study to try to answer the question of what goes wrong when Lyme disease simply will not go away.

2

The Discovery of Lyme Disease

For the discovery of Lyme disease, society owes as much gratitude to two mothers as it does to any doctors or medical researchers. Those two concerned mothers are Polly Murray and Judith Mensch. These women called attention to the outbreak of arthritis that was sweeping their Connecticut communities.[1] Polly Murray, a mother of four and an artist, noticed a major outbreak of arthritis in and around the town of Lyme, Connecticut, in 1975. Strangely, the arthritis—usually found only in older people—was affecting children. Twelve children—in a town of just five thousand people—had swollen joints or were on crutches. Most of those children had been diagnosed as having juvenile rheumatoid arthritis, a very rare disease. She brought this outbreak to the attention of the state medical authorities. They then contacted Yale University, and Dr. Allen Steere began an investigation that eventually led to the discovery of the bacteria causing the disease. Before this time, though, what we now call Lyme disease was not well known in the United States. This lack of medical knowledge made life very difficult for Mrs. Murray, her family, the people of Lyme, and everyone else living where this puzzling disease was flourishing.

Life in the Country

The Murrays had moved to the Lyme, Connecticut, area in the late 1950s. They had left behind the noise and congestion of New York City for a house along a quiet, isolated road, surrounded by woods. In the summer of 1963, Mrs. Murray was pregnant with her fourth child. One day she came into the house from the garden. It was a steamy hot day, and she was looking forward to cooling off with a glass of iced tea. Her son David took one look at her and said, "Mom, your face looks funny."[2] Sure enough, when she looked in the mirror, she saw a strange red streak on her chin and neck. Later, she felt achy and had a fever. When she visited her doctor, he called the rash an expanding bacterial skin infection, which in a way it was. He put her on penicillin, and she began to feel better. Still, she felt terribly fatigued for the rest of her pregnancy. She would later look back on this incident and recognize that it was her earliest brush with Lyme disease. Over the years, Mrs. Murray and her family would have many bouts of this mystery ailment.

In October 1974, her son Sandy, who was seventeen years old and captain of the soccer team, became ill. He was away at boarding school and woke up one morning with unexplained stiffness and pain in his neck and shoulders. Then he had pain in his legs and began to limp.

Mrs. Murray herself had bouts of rashes and pain, as did her other children and her husband. When she talked about it to others, she found she was not alone. At a dinner party that fall, she described her family's woes to a friend who lived in a nearby town. Her friend said that her daughter also had had a fever and painful joints. Another friend reported a rash on her daughter's hands. Still another acquaintance had suddenly become quite tired and developed arthritis. Something was clearly wrong in Lyme, but what was it?

In June 1975, Mrs. Murray got a call from the school nurse about her eleven-year-old son, Todd. He had a welt and round rash on his left arm. By August, both Todd and Sandy had knees so swollen they could not even walk. Doctors did not know what to make of these symptoms, especially in two brothers at the same time. Most of them were baffled. Some doctors suggested she was making it all up. In fact, one doctor came right out and said, "I suppose you think this is some new disease. Why, they might even call it Murray's disease."[3]

By October 1975, Mrs. Murray was frantic to find an answer to her family's problems. She called the Connecticut State Health Department, which took down her information and promised to call her back. In the meantime, she got on the telephone and began doing a bit of detective work of her own. By calling many people in her town, she was able to develop a list of sufferers.

Polly Murray helped bring an outbreak of arthritis in children to the attention of authorities.

In November, another concerned mother, Judith Mensch, had also called the state health department and reported that four children on her block alone, including her own eight-year-old daughter, Anne, had painful swollen joints.

The Yale Investigation

Finally, the case was taken seriously by Dr. David Snydman at the Connecticut State Health Department, who said, "I didn't know what it was, but it sounded interesting." He passed the information along to a friend of his, Dr. Allen Steere, a specialist in joint diseases at Yale University, who also took the outbreak quite seriously. "What's happening in Lyme is unheard of," he said in 1977. Dr. Steere set aside his other laboratory work to get to the bottom of this outbreak of arthritis.[4]

Dr. Steere and other medical researchers spent the next two years carefully studying the disease, which they named "Lyme disease" after the place where it was discovered. The doctors found the arthritis in a total of 39 children and 12 adults in the Lyme area of Connecticut. Thirteen of those people remembered having gotten a circular rash before they got the arthritis. The doctors knew that such a rash could be caused by a tick bite. The medical researchers looked for ticks by dragging the bushes in the area with white cloth, onto which the ticks drop. They found that the most common species was the minute deer tick, *Ixodes scapularis*. This tick is about the size of a poppy seed and is usually not noticed until after it has latched onto the skin and drunk its fill of blood.

Deer ticks (*Ixodes scapularis*) carry Lyme disease in the Northeast and Midwest.

Simply knowing which insect was carrying Lyme disease, however, did not bring Dr. Steere and his associates any closer to finding the actual bacteria or to developing a cure. Unfortunately, they became convinced that this was a whole new disease never seen before. As we will see later in this chapter, this was not the case. They also came to believe that Lyme disease was caused by a virus. Researchers spent the next several years in a fruitless search for the right virus.

A Lucky Accident

As so often happens in science, the discovery of the bacteria that cause Lyme disease happened almost by accident. Willy

Burgdorfer, a scientist at the Rocky Mountain Laboratories in Hamilton, Montana, was hoping to find the cause of a particularly nasty outbreak of Rocky Mountain spotted fever on Long Island, New York.[5] Rocky Mountain spotted fever is another disease carried by ticks, but it is caused by a rickettsia, a single-celled parasite that looks a lot like a bacterium. As its name implies, this disease causes a person to break out in red spots, and it can be fatal.

Burgdorfer was a specialist in dissecting all sorts of tiny insects. In the fall of 1981, he went to work with his miniature scalpels, gently taking Long Island ticks apart and searching for microbes. However, he could not find any rickettsia that would explain the deaths from Rocky Mountain spotted fever. On a hunch, he switched to dissecting deer ticks, which are the most common species of tick on Long Island. Again, he failed to find the spotted fever rickettsia. But in a couple of the ticks he found something unexpected—tiny spiral-shaped bacteria called spirochetes. He knew that spirochetes do not cause Rocky Mountain spotted fever, but they do cause other diseases, syphilis for one. At this point, he knew he was onto something big.[6]

Right away, he got together with one of his co-workers at the Rocky Mountain Labs, Dr. Alan Barbour. They began filtering antibodies from the blood of Lyme disease patients. Antibodies are proteins that the body's immune system makes when it is attacked by bacteria and viruses. These proteins stick to the surface of bacteria and help the immune system destroy them. They discovered that the antibodies in the blood of Lyme disease patients stuck to the spirochetes that came from the deer ticks. This discovery meant they had found the right bacteria that cause Lyme disease. From there other researchers, including Dr. Allen Steere, were able to confirm that other patients with Lyme disease were also infected with the same type of spirochete. In 1984 the bacterium was dubbed *Borrelia burgdorferi,* to honor Dr. Burgdorfer's efforts.

Not a New Disease

Lyme disease was not a brand-new disease. European doctors had known about it since early in the twentieth century. The problem was that they had been calling it something else. In 1909 in Sweden, Dr. Arvid Afzelius showed a group of his fellow dermatologists the case of an elderly woman who had an odd bull's-eye rash. The rash had started as a red circle at the spot where she was bitten by a sheep tick. Over several days, he had seen the circle spread outward. Because the rash was on the move, he called it *erythema migrans,* meaning "migrating redness." In 1913 in Austria, Dr. B. Lipschütz noticed that the rashes lasted a long time, sometimes as long as seven months. This was far longer than any ordinary rash. So he changed the name to *erythema chronicum migrans,* with the word *chronicum* meaning "chronic" or "long term." To make it easier, they usually referred to the skin disease by its initials, ECM.

In those days, it was well known that ticks were spreading the disease, but no one knew for sure what the ticks were carrying. Dr. Lipschütz was quite sure it was bacteria. He proposed that if

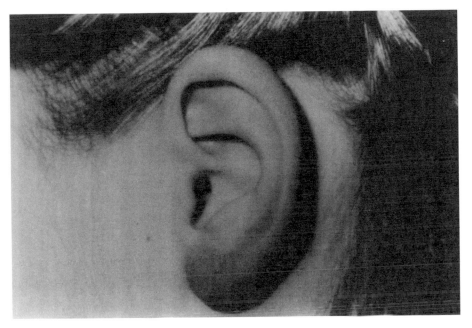

A bite from an infected tick produced this red swollen rash on the earlobe.

someone dissected ticks and searched their intestines and salivary glands under a microscope, they might find the bacteria. However, no one took his advice, and the discovery of the Lyme disease bacterium was put on hold for almost seventy years.

The idea that ECM was being caused by bacteria got a boost in Europe in 1955. In a courageous but dangerous experiment, Dr. H. Gotz and four other researchers used themselves as human guinea pigs. They took a bit of skin from the rash of a patient with ECM and injected it into their own skin. Each one of them developed the rash. They then cured it with the antibiotic penicillin. Their experiment showed that ECM was caused by an infection, not a rash or other skin irritation.

The cause and cure for ECM were now established. So why was Lyme disease so hard for doctors to diagnose in 1975? The reason is that European researchers had focused on the skin-rash symptom of the disease, but the people in Lyme, Connecticut, were having problems with their joints. This was enough to throw the doctors off track. They did not realize that they were dealing with the same disease. Instead of concentrating on bacteria, they searched high and low for a virus. Why did they look for a virus? In the 1970s, it was thought that most of the bacteria that infect humans had already been discovered. Viruses, on the other hand, were the hot topic of the day. So they concentrated their efforts on searching for a virus.[7]

Willy Burgdorfer, who was originally from Switzerland, was familiar with the work going on in Europe with ECM rashes. He also recalled that arthritis was occasionally seen in patients with ECM. That is why, when he cut into the deer ticks and found spirochetes, he said to himself, "Oh boy, I've really found something."[8] He finally had the right combination of skills and knowledge to put all the facts together and discover the right answer.

An Emerging Disease

Lyme disease is what the Centers for Disease Control (CDC) calls an emerging disease—a disease that was once rare or unknown, but is becoming much more common. Remember, it was only in 1975 that the epidemic of arthritis in Lyme, Connecticut, was first brought to the attention of health authorities. At that time, only a few dozen people were thought to be infected. In 1982, 497 cases of Lyme disease were reported to the CDC. In 1995, just thirteen years later, the number of reported cases jumped to 11,603. In 1996 a record-high 16,461 cases nationwide were reported.[9] Today the disease is concentrated in the northeastern states of New York, Connecticut, Pennsylvania, New Jersey, Rhode Island, Maryland, Massachusetts, and Delaware. Many cases have also been reported in Wisconsin, Minnesota, and California. In fact, Lyme disease can now be found in 45 of the 50 states. Where did this new disease originally come from?

Some scientists have speculated that the disease was brought fairly recently from Europe, perhaps with imported sheep.[10] New research suggests that the disease has been around for at least one hundred years. To find out just how long ago Lyme disease existed in North America, a group of scientists took a look at museum specimens of white-footed mice, which are known to carry the bacteria that cause Lyme disease. In all, they examined 280 mice and other small rodents that had been collected during the late 1800s and early 1900s and were stored at the Smithsonian Institution in Washington, D.C., the American Museum of Natural History in New York City, and at Harvard University's Museum of Comparative Zoology in Boston.[11]

How do you go about finding bacteria in one-hundred-year-old, dried-up mice? You don't. Instead, the scientists looked for remnants of the bacteria's genes. This is almost the same way that fictional researchers in the movie *Jurassic Park* hunted through fossils for dinosaur DNA. In a way, DNA works like a computer program. But instead of using bits and bytes, DNA carries chemical codes in a genetic program that tell the cells what to do.

The researchers took snips out of the mouse ears and broke down the cells to free the DNA inside. Then they added an enzyme called DNA polymerase. Enzymes are proteins that perform special functions inside the body. The function of the DNA polymerase is to make exact copies of any DNA it comes across, including the DNA from the Lyme disease bacteria. The researchers found what they were looking for. Two of the mice skin samples contained the bacteria's genes. This meant that when the mice were collected one hundred years ago, they had to have been infected with the Lyme disease bacteria. Both specimens had been collected in 1894 from the Cape Cod town of Dennis, Massachusetts, proving that mice carrying the disease had been in America for at least one hundred years. German researchers repeated the procedure, this time working with museum specimens of ticks. The scientists showed that the bacteria were in European ticks as early as 1884.[12]

If the Lyme disease bacteria have been around all this time, why was it only in 1975 that the big outbreak in Lyme, Connecticut, occurred? The answer seems to be forests. Deep forests have come back to the Northeast in recent years. American Indians were known to keep the land clear of excess

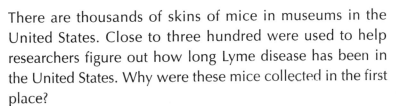

What Good Are Dried-Up Old Mice?

There are thousands of skins of mice in museums in the United States. Close to three hundred were used to help researchers figure out how long Lyme disease has been in the United States. Why were these mice collected in the first place?

Zoologists began collecting many animal specimens in the late 1800s. They would take off on great expeditions into the wilds of Africa, Asia, and North America, collecting every type of mammal, bird, and insect they encountered. This was shortly after Charles Darwin began writing about the origin of species and the theory of evolution. The collections were used to help classify animals by order, genus, and species. Because individual animals differ in size, weight, and coloring, the collectors would bring in dozens of examples of each species.

Among the animal collectors was Otram Bangs, who later became the curator of Harvard University's Museum of Comparative Zoology. In all, he donated about ten thousand of his own specimens to the museum. Many years later, forty-one of his mice were used in the study of the origins of Lyme disease.

Instead of storing an entire animal, Bangs and other collectors would skin them, then dust the skin with a powdered mixture of arsenic, borax, and alum (a salt) to prevent decay. They would then stuff the skins with cotton.[13]

Even these immaculately kept grounds can harbor Lyme disease-carrying ticks.

brush and small trees by periodically burning the forests and meadows.[14] When the European settlers moved in, they chopped down much of the forest to get firewood and to clear land for pastures and farms. As a result, the Northeast lost much of its forests. In addition, the white-tailed deer, which carry the ticks and prefer the edge of the forest, became nearly extinct.

As small farms in the Northeast became less profitable during the twentieth century, they were gradually abandoned and the forests grew back. This gave the deer plenty of trees and brush for cover. The population of white-tailed deer grew dramatically, especially in the 1970s when Lyme disease suddenly burst upon the scene. At the same time, more and more people were escaping the big cities and building new homes near these newly regrown, deer-rich forests. The result was a dramatic outbreak of Lyme disease, an outbreak that continues to this day.

3

What Is Lyme Disease?

Lyme disease is caused by spiral-shaped bacteria called *Borrelia burgdorferi*. Bacteria are different from viruses. Viruses are simply long strings of genetic material that are enclosed inside a protective protein shell. They cannot live on their own outside of a living host organism because they cannot produce the biochemicals, such as enzymes, that are needed to break down and use food. Viruses also cannot reproduce by themselves. In order to reproduce, they must invade a cell and hijack its biological machinery.

Bacteria such as *B. burgdorferi* can reproduce themselves. They can also absorb nutrients from the surrounding environment and break them down for energy. Bacteria may become specialized, though. For instance, when you add certain bacteria to milk, they break down the milk sugar (lactose) into lactic acid. The result is yogurt. Lyme disease bacteria, however, do not live in milk. Instead, they depend on the blood of animals to provide a safe, warm, protected environment full of the sugars and amino acids they need to live and grow. As a result, *B. burgdorferi* bacteria do not live for very long in soil or water. Instead, they must be passed directly from animals to ticks and then to other animals in order for new generations to survive. But with so many ticks and animal hosts around, this is not a problem.

From Mice to Ticks to People

Lyme disease does not travel in the air, in water, in food, or in any of the usual ways that other viruses and bacteria can infect you. Instead, ticks spread the disease from animals to people. Deer ticks are called "vectors" because they carry Lyme disease–causing bacteria but are never made ill by the infection. Another example of a vector is the mosquito that carries the parasite that causes malaria.

Once kind of tick in particular, the deer tick, also known by its scientific name *Ixodes scapularis,* is the usual carrier of Lyme disease. When the ticks are young, they are difficult to see and remove from the body.

Although Lyme disease can be a terrible illness, especially if not caught early, humans are not a good place for *B. burgdorferi* to survive and be passed on to other animals. This is because people are less likely than animals to develop the infection and then be bitten by uninfected ticks who would pass on the bacteria to still more animals. When the bacteria reach people, they die out.

Many kinds of animals can be infected with the bacteria. These include not only deer, but also birds, dogs, raccoons, squirrels, and mice. The animals that are probably the most important for the tick's life cycle, and thus for the cycle of Lyme disease, are the white-footed mouse and the white-tailed deer.

The ticks that carry Lyme disease live about two years.[1] In the spring, the female tick lays her eggs among the leaves and debris on the ground. The larvae hatch in the summer. Even if their parents were infected with *B. burgdorferi*, the larvae are almost always born free of the bacteria. They usually spend their summer feasting on the blood of a mouse or other small animal. If the mouse is infected with *B. burgdorferi*, the bacteria can pass from the mouse's blood into the larvae's gut. Although the tick plays an important role in carrying the disease to others, the mouse is equally vital in this chain because it acts as a safe haven, what scientists call a reservoir, for the bacteria. After the larvae have engorged themselves with blood, they drop off the mouse.

In the next stage of life the deer tick larvae grow larger, getting to about the size of a poppy seed. They are now called nymphs. They spend the winter without feeding. Springtime is the most dangerous time for people because with the warmer weather the nymphs become active. Many of these nymphs may now be infected with the Lyme disease bacteria from the previous year's feast on mouse blood. They crawl onto bushes and grass in the hopes of brushing onto a passing animal and getting a blood meal.

In areas of the country where Lyme disease is prevalent, up to 25 percent of the nymphs are infected with *B. burgdorferi.* In fact, it is the nymphs, not the adults ticks, that are responsible for 90 percent of the Lyme disease cases in people. This is because of their small size, their greater numbers, and their high level of activity in the spring and summer, when people are just getting out and enjoying nature.

Once a nymph has filled itself with blood for three to four days, it drops off the animal. It then begins growing into an adult. The adult deer ticks, which are about the size of a sesame seed, are easier to spot crawling around on your clothes or burrowed into your skin. Actually, if an infected tick is

Life Cycle of *Ixodes scapularis* Tick

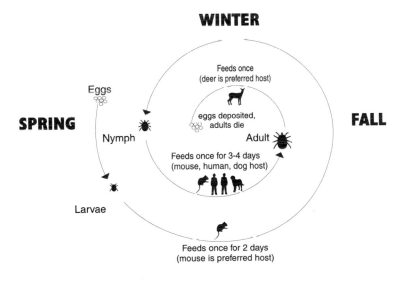

WINTER

Feeds once
(deer is preferred host)

Eggs

eggs deposited,
adults die

SPRING

Nymph

Adult

FALL

Feeds once for 3-4 days
(mouse, human, dog host)

Larvae

Feeds once for 2 days
(mouse is preferred host)

SUMMER

The life cycle of the deer tick is about two years.

found within a day or two and properly removed, it will probably not pass on the bacteria. This is because the bacteria live deep within the tick's digestive tract and it takes a while for them to migrate to the tick's mouth.

Adult ticks are also less of a hazard because they only start to seek out an animal host for a last blood meal before winter, usually as cooler weather approaches in mid-October. This is also the same time when people begin to make fewer trips into the countryside. So, even though as many as half of all adult deer ticks carry the bacteria, they are only responsible for about 10 percent of the cases of Lyme disease in people.

Of the adult deer ticks, only the females seek out an animal or a person for a blood meal. They use this blood to nurture their eggs, which they lay in the spring. This starts the cycle all over again. Deer are the animals of choice for adult deer ticks to feed on. First of all, deer are abundant. Second, they are roaming about the forests and meadows at the same time that the ticks are looking for a meal. Thus, many deer become infected with the Lyme disease bacteria. The deer do not transfer the disease to uninfected ticks or to other species. All the deer do is provide a moving feast for the adult female ticks. This feast then enables the females to lay the eggs that launch the next round of nymphs.

Clearly, both mice and deer are required to provide a steady supply of bacteria to keep the cycle of Lyme disease going—the mice for larvae, and the deer to give adult female ticks a final feeding ground. This is why Lyme disease is prevalent only in certain areas of the country. It has to be a place where there are plenty of mice, deer, and deer ticks, all near to where people live, play, or work.

The Tick Bite

When a deer tick bites a person, it does not mean that the person will necessarily develop Lyme disease. First, the tick must be infected with the Lyme disease bacteria. The number of ticks that carry the *Borrelia burgdorferi* bacteria varies from region to region. In some parts of the country, less than one percent of the ticks are infected, while in other parts as many as 70 percent are infected. Although the deer tick carries *B. burgdorferi*, researchers do not think that the

White-tailed deer provide a blood meal for adult female deer ticks in the fall. This meal provides nourishment for the female ticks and allows them to lay eggs in the spring.

ticks themselves become sick with Lyme disease. This means that the disease-carrying ticks are just as active and just as likely to land on you and bite you.

Once a tick has landed on skin, it hunts around for a safe place to burrow. This is why ticks are often found along the edge of the hairline or in folds like the armpits or behind the knees. Before digging in for a meal, the tick injects a chemical, very much like the Novocain a dentist uses, into the skin to numb any feeling of pain. Then it punches through the skin with its proboscis, a sharp snout with barbs on it, until it hits a capillary. At that point, the tick begins sucking blood. The bacteria that cause Lyme disease usually live deep inside the tick's digestive tract, so they are not passed from the tick into the skin instantly. It may be a day or two after the tick has burrowed into the skin before it passes along the infection. This is why it is important to search for and remove ticks promptly. The proper removal process will be described in detail in Chapter 7. Once the bacteria make their way from the gut to the mouth of the tick, as happens during the feeding process, they enter the person's skin and the infection begins.

After the Bite

Once the bacteria that cause Lyme disease have entered the skin through the tick bite, the person or animal usually becomes infected. Between 60 and 80 percent of people who are infected with the Lyme disease bacteria get a peculiar rash that usually starts at the place where the tick was attached. This rash appears anywhere from three to thirty days after the tick burrows in. Because the ticks are so small, most people never even know they were bitten. So the rash is usually the first thing they see.[2]

The rash usually begins as a bump at the spot where the tick was attached. Then, over the next few days or weeks, a red circular patch keeps growing bigger as the bacteria, like an invading army, move outward into new, uninfected skin. The

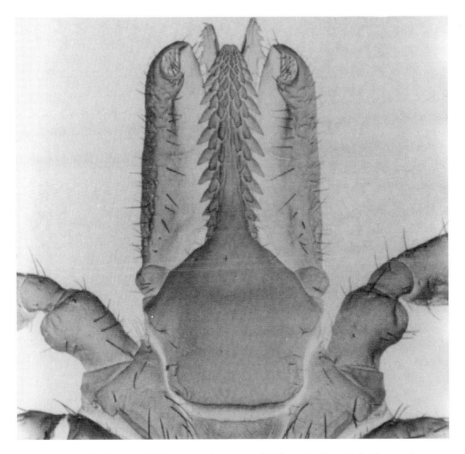

A magnified view of the mouth parts of a female deer tick shows the barbs on the inner mouth parts. These allow the tick to make a firm connection to the skin.

redness and swelling of the rash are caused by increased blood flow to the area as the body tries to fight the infection.

Even in the early stage of Lyme disease, the bacteria can leave the skin and enter the bloodstream. From there, they can move to other areas of the skin, producing many rashes. The bacteria can also enter the eye, causing redness and irritation called conjunctivitis. If the bacteria get into the nervous system, the result can be Bell's palsy. In this case, half of the face looks strangely frozen, and the person can manage to give only half a smile. This is because the bacteria have infected the nerves on one side of the face. Occasionally, both sides of the face are affected. It is a kind of temporary paralysis that will go away within about a month, even if it is not treated with antibiotics. Of course, it will disappear faster if properly treated.

Other frequent symptoms of early Lyme disease are low fever and chills, joint and muscle pains, headaches, and fatigue. All of these symptoms can be mistaken for the flu. The big difference is that there is no coughing or sneezing involved, as you would expect with the flu. In regions where Lyme disease is common, a summer or early-fall bout with "the flu" is a good reason to visit the doctor.

Fortunately, much has been learned about Lyme disease. Doctors and people living in areas where the disease is common have been taught to avoid ticks and to recognize the symptoms. Currently, 90 percent of adults and children who become infected are diagnosed when the disease is still in its early stage. Almost all of these people respond to the standard antibiotic therapy and have no future problems.

Untreated Lyme Disease

Most people never see or feel the tick that bites them. Some never get the rash, and others get the rash but simply ignore it. If a person infected with the Lyme disease bacteria fails to get antibiotic treatment within a few weeks of the first bite, the disease can spread to other parts of the body, specifically the brain, heart, and joints. This is called second-stage Lyme disease.[3] Second-stage Lyme disease is curable, but it takes longer to eliminate the bacteria. Arthritis is the most common second-stage symptom of Lyme disease. The knees will often swell so badly that crutches may be needed. As we have already learned, it was children with arthritis, not rashes, that originally alerted medical investigators to the disease.

The brain may become badly affected anywhere from one month to fourteen years after the tick bite. Headaches, fatigue, and constant sleepiness may occur. Second-stage Lyme disease can affect people's memory and concentration. It can also make them cranky and moody.

Other Diseases Carried by Ticks

In the United States, Lyme disease has become the most common human disease carried by ticks or any other insect. The publicity surrounding Lyme disease has drawn attention to other, less common diseases that are also carried by ticks.

About eight hundred species of ticks are found in the world, and of these, almost one hundred species can infect people with bacteria, viruses, or protozoa.[4] Some of the illnesses carried by ticks are listed on page 41.

The same deer tick that infects people with Lyme disease can also carry microscopic parasites called *Babesia microti.* These parasites are protozoa—single-celled creatures. Protozoa are the simplest form of animal life. Malaria, for instance, is caused by protozoa that are carried by mosquitoes.

Research shows that about 10 percent of people diagnosed with Lyme disease in southern New England also have the *Babesia microti* protozoa.[5] They probably were infected by the same tick that gave them Lyme disease. On their own, the protozoa cause a flulike illness called babesiosis. When you get babesiosis along with Lyme disease, however, the symptoms of both are made much worse. Also, babesiosis can occasionally be fatal. Whereas Lyme disease can usually be cured with antibiotics alone, babesiosis must be treated with additional drugs such as quinine, the same drug used against malaria. Whenever a patient has a case of Lyme disease that is especially serious or just does not get better, doctors are cautioned to look for signs of babesiosis.

Human granulocytic ehrlichiosis (HGE) is another recently identified illness carried by ticks.[7] The bacteria that cause it, which have not been named yet, can be found not only in deer ticks but also in brown dog ticks. The disease is found in many of the same parts of the Northeast where Lyme disease is found. The disease attacks blood cells and the liver,

Some of the Major Tick-Borne Illnesses of the World[6]

Caused by Bacteria
Lyme disease
Rocky Mountain spotted fever
human granulocytic ehrlichiosis (HGE)
ehrlichiosis
tularemia
Q fever
relapsing fever
Japanese spotted fever
Queensland tick typhus fever
Siberian tick typhus

Caused by Protozoa
babesiosis

Caused by Viruses
Powassan fever
Kyasanur Forest disease
Thogota infection
Congo-Crimean hemorrhagic fever
Louping ill virus fever
Russian spring-summer encephalitis

Grass and brush at the edge of a forest are the deer tick's favorite hiding place.

causing severe fever, headaches, and vomiting. It is treated with antibiotics.

Rocky Mountain spotted fever can be found not only in mountainous states like Montana, Colorado, and North Carolina but also in Oklahoma and even New York City. It is carried by dog ticks and mountain wood ticks. The adult female ticks infect people with bacteria called *Rickettsia rickettsii.* Instead of one big rash, the body is often covered with little red spots, hence, the name spotted fever. There are also headaches, fever, and muscle and joint pains. Because it is caused by bacteria, Rocky Mountain spotted fever can be cured with antibiotics. It is a very dangerous illness if not caught and treated within two weeks. It can be fatal to 25 percent of the people who fail to get treatment.

4

Diagnosing Lyme Disease

John Green, a fifty-one-year-old writer and video producer living in suburban Connecticut, noticed a tiny tick burrowed into the skin of his upper arm one day. The skin around the tick was a bit swollen and red, and the tick itself was full of blood. "Darn," he grumbled. "If this turns into Lyme disease, I'll be mighty annoyed."[1]

He got out his tweezers, and grasping the tick as close to the skin as possible, he gently pulled it out, put it into the toilet, and flushed. He hoped that was the last he would see of that pesky critter.

Nine days later, he found a small red circle at the spot where the tick had bitten him. The circle grew into a rash that got bigger and bigger each day until it looked like a bull's-eye. The odd-looking rash was hot, and it felt incredibly itchy and sore. He did not immediately suspect Lyme disease because he had always heard that the rash it causes is painless. Still, he decided to go to his doctor just to make sure.

Because Green lived in the part of Connecticut with the highest rate of Lyme disease in the United States, the doctors had seen many cases just like his. When Green took off his shirt, showing the rash and then describing the tick bite, his doctor was immediately convinced that this was Lyme disease. Green was puzzled, though. Didn't the doctor need to draw blood? Shouldn't he do a test to be sure? Curiously, the answer Green got was no.

As his doctor explained, Lyme disease is not like a sore throat. With sore throats, there are lots of bacteria swarming about on the surface of the throat. A doctor can simply do a throat culture to get a sample of them to grow in culture on a petri dish. Then the doctor can easily identify the bacteria causing the illness. It is easy to grow the streptococcus bacteria that cause strep throat, but the Lyme disease bacteria are much trickier. A doctor would have to cut out a portion of the skin where the rash is to see if the bacteria are there. Not only would it be painful, but there would still be a chance that the test would come up negative, even though the person is actually infected.

Another approach is to take a blood sample and look for antibodies. Antibodies are large proteins that the body's immune system creates when it is infected. These proteins seek out bacteria and viruses, stick to them, and then help the body's immune system destroy them. It takes a while for the body to start producing antibodies to bacteria. In the early stages of Lyme disease there might not be a large enough amount of the antibodies for the blood test to detect. For instance, eight days after being bitten by an infected tick, only 40 percent of the people with Lyme disease have enough antibodies in their blood for the disease to be detected. So an early test often comes back negative. This is called a false negative because it failed to detect the infection that is present in the patient's body. Six weeks after infection, though, almost everyone who is infected will test positive. Antibodies, and the blood tests to detect them, are described in more detail later in this chapter.

Doctors Diagnose from Symptoms

Actually, this was not the first time John Green had encountered Lyme disease. A few years earlier, he had a fever and chills more severe than anything he had ever experienced. Just before this earlier episode, he had seen a tick on his skin but never got the rash. Because Green did not have the usual rash, the doctor ordered a blood test. It came back negative, but the doctor said that a false negative is not unusual in the early stages of Lyme disease. Based on the symptoms and the fact that Lyme disease was so common in the area, the doctor was convinced that Green had Lyme disease and should start on antibiotics right away. The doctor felt it was better to be cautious than to risk the serious consequences of not treating the disease early.[2]

Studies show that, early in the disease, only about one third of children and adults with a single bull's-eye rash will actually test positive for Lyme disease.[3] For this reason, doctors are urged not to rely entirely on tests, but instead to look for the symptoms of Lyme disease, such as the rash or facial paralysis.[4] In its early stages, the disease is so mild and so easily cured with antibiotics that it is not worth waiting for the blood test to turn positive to confirm the diagnosis. By the time the test turns positive, the bacteria may already be causing joint and nervous system problems.

Symptoms of Lyme Disease

The most common symptom of Lyme disease is the bull's-eye rash. In a study of Connecticut children newly diagnosed with Lyme disease, 66 percent had only one rash, 28 percent had more than one, and 6 percent had arthritis.[5] In some cases, people just get flulike symptoms with a high fever and chills. What is different about these flu symptoms is that there is no runny nose and cough. Also, the symptoms usually come in the summer or early fall, which is not the usual time to get the flu. Other patients show up at their doctor's offices with Bell's palsy, a paralysis of the major nerve running down the side of the face. The Lyme disease bacteria can cause Bell's palsy, but so can other bacteria and viruses. So Bell's palsy alone is not enough to convince a doctor that it is Lyme disease.

The most common symptom is, of course, the rash. The expanding Lyme disease rash can be round or oval-shaped and usually grows to about six inches across, although it can grow to as large as twelve inches or more. As the rash gets larger, the skin closest to the tick bite clears up, which makes the rash look a bit like a bull's-eye. The rash is usually warm to the

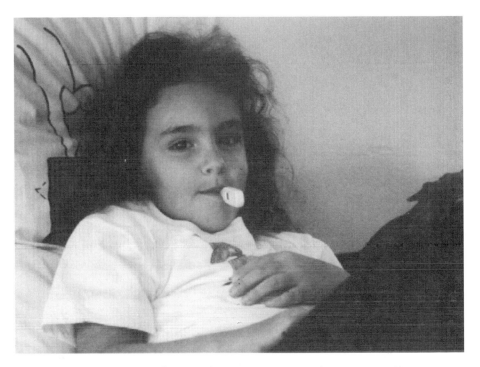

A child with a high fever in the summertime, without any respiratory symptoms, may have Lyme disease.

touch, and it might be a bit itchy, but it usually is not painful. Besides having the rash, a person with Lyme disease might also be tired and have a headache, stiff neck, and muscle or joint pains.

The rash will go away on its own within a few days or weeks, even without the standard antibiotic treatment. As mentioned earlier, only a third of people who have a single rash will test positive for Lyme disease. So, if you see a mysterious round rash and you live in or have visited a place where Lyme disease is common, show it to your doctor right away. After the rash vanishes, the disease may go into hiding and reemerge as arthritis or other symptoms of second-stage Lyme disease.

Blood Tests for Detecting Lyme Disease

Without the help of antibiotics, your body cannot rid itself completely of Lyme disease bacteria. The body is not entirely helpless, however. As with any other infection, the immune system attacks the bacterial invaders. One of the first lines of attack is the antibodies, which are proteins produced by white blood cells (WBCs). There are about two trillion WBCs in the body, and they are always on guard against infection.[6]

When WBCs stumble across a bacterium, they search all over its surface until they find a protein that is found only on that particular kind of bacterium. To picture how the cell makes antibodies to this protein, imagine closing your eyes and feeling around inside a sack full of balls. The baseball has stitches on its surface, the golf ball has its dimples, the basketball has tiny bumps, and the bowling ball is mostly smooth but has three holes for the fingers. Now imagine pressing a piece of clay against the golf ball. When you gently peel away the clay and pull it out of the sack, what do you see? It is an exact copy of the pattern on the golf ball, only its opposite. Instead of dimples, the clay has bumps that fit the pattern of the golf ball. If you hand that piece of clay to a friend, he or she could use it to find the golf ball again, just by matching the patterns.

This is something like what your body does when it fights infection. Only instead of clay, your body creates antibodies out of proteins. Plus, it has another trick. At the other end of the antibody it tacks on a tail. This tail is like a red flag that signals passing WBCs to gulp down the bacterium and rip it apart with a deadly mix of enzymes and corrosive chemicals like hydrogen peroxide.

Once the WBCs encounter bacteria, they continue to dump antibodies into the blood in the hope that they will bump into the bacteria, attach to them, and sound the alert. These free-floating antibodies can be detected with a blood test called ELISA (enzyme-linked immunosorbent assay).[7]

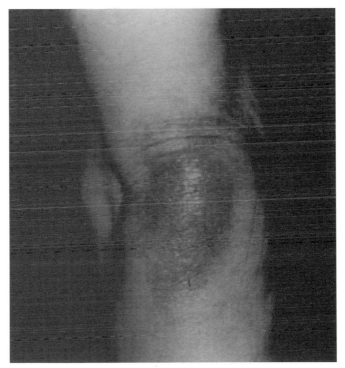

A knee is shown with the swelling and redness of Lyme disease.

Antibody tests are most useful in cases where the characteristic bull's-eye rash is missing and after the infection has been present for several weeks, when plenty of antibodies are available.

The difficulty in using blood tests to detect Lyme disease is that it takes a month or so before there are enough antibodies in the bloodstream to be detected. During this time, the ELISA test might give a false-negative result. That is, it may fail to detect the infection, even though it is there. After six to eight weeks of infection, the bacteria have migrated to other parts of the body and the antibody production really gets going.

What Doctors Look For in Diagnosing Lyme Disease

- A report of a bite from a small tick
- Living in or visiting a Lyme disease area
- A round or oval-shaped rash, often clear in the middle like a bull's-eye (the best indicator)
- Fever and chills
- Headache, fatigue, and memory problems
- Bell's palsy, i.e., facial paralysis
- Pain and swelling of joints
- Fainting spells, caused by irregular or slow heartbeat
- A positive blood test for *Borrelia burgdorferi* bacteria

A blood test for antibodies can also give a false-positive result. The false positive usually happens when a person still has antibodies in the blood, even after a past infection has cleared up. A person might also be infected with different bacteria that have proteins similar to the ones that cause Lyme disease. The bacteria that cause syphilis will give a false positive for Lyme disease in the ELISA test, for instance. Because of the chance of false positives, another test, the Western blot, is used.

In the Western blot, a patient's blood sample is placed on a piece of blotting paper. The blotting paper already contains a number of different-sized Lyme disease bacteria proteins in the paper. If the patient's blood sample has antibodies for Lyme disease, they will show up when applied to the paper. The test is considered positive if the blood reacts to at least five of the ten characteristic Lyme disease proteins on the paper.

Difficulties In Diagnosing Lyme Disease

Anytime a new disease is identified, there is a tendency to look for it everywhere and to blame it for a wide variety of woes, some real and some imagined. Lyme disease is no different in that regard. Before Lyme disease was identified, many people who had it did not know it, and were never treated for it. Nowadays, though, with the growing awareness of the disease, the tendency is for doctors to treat it anytime it is suspected.[8] But there are problems with this approach. First, it means that some patients are taking antibiotics for a disease they do not have. A more serious problem occurs when patients are falsely

51

treated for Lyme disease when another disease is actually causing their ill health and going untreated.

At the University of Connecticut Health Center (UCHC), medical researchers wanted to find out how often doctors either treat Lyme disease in patients who do not actually have it, or fail to treat Lyme disease in patients who really do have it. The researchers looked at the medical records of 146 children between the ages of two and twenty-one. These children had some of the symptoms of Lyme disease and had been sent to the health center by their family doctor.[9]

The researchers found that only about 60 percent of the children actually had Lyme disease; the others did not. For example, thirteen of the patients had rashlike skin problems resulting from fungus infections, eczema, poison ivy, or allergic reactions. Others with headaches, fatigue, joint pains, or heart problems had also been incorrectly diagnosed with Lyme disease.

On the other hand, five patients had the opposite problem. They had real Lyme disease rashes that their doctors misidentified as something else. In three of these patients, the rash had faded in just three to four days, and because most Lyme rashes last two weeks or more, their family doctors had assumed it was not really Lyme disease. Another child's rash was misidentified as a streptococcus bacteria infection, rather than Lyme disease, because it was painful. But as we have already seen in John Green's case, the Lyme disease rash can sometimes be painful. Another child's rash was not clear in the middle, leading the original doctor to conclude it was not a Lyme disease rash. At the UCHC clinic, however, all five children tested positive for Lyme disease with the ELISA blood test.

The doctors who conducted the UCHC study concluded that Lyme disease is being overdiagnosed in 38 percent of patients.[10] On the other hand, about 8 percent of patients who actually have the disease are not being properly diagnosed and treated. Medical researchers are hoping to reduce the rate of misdiagnosis by developing better blood tests and educating doctors in the correct diagnosis and treatment of Lyme disease.

5

Treating Lyme Disease

Jona is now a fourteen-year-old girl in the ninth grade. She lives in a rural area outside Groton, Connecticut. From time to time she even sees deer grazing on the lawn or nibbling their bushes. She is also an avid soccer player and loves to ride her bike and jog along the trails of the nearby state park. Four years ago, she had an encounter with one of the creatures out there, a deer tick. She never saw it, which is usually the case, but she felt the effects of its bite about a week later. "I kind of didn't really feel like myself," she said. "I had a fever, and my muscles ached a lot. But I didn't see a rash."[1] Sure enough, though, within a couple more days she saw a big round rash on her leg. It was red on the outside and clear in the middle. As soon as her mother saw that rash, she took Jona to show it to the doctor. He took a look at it, but also asked other questions. Had she been outdoors a lot and had she been having fever, chills, and muscle or joint pains? When she answered yes to those questions, he decided it must be Lyme disease. He did not order any blood tests, and gave her an oral antibiotic called amoxicillin. She took that three times a day for three weeks, and has felt fine ever since.

Jona's case of Lyme disease is typical. About 90 percent of people find out quickly what it is, and are given antibiotics to be taken by mouth. That is all that is usually needed to wipe out the bacteria. Not everyone is as lucky as Jona, though.

Heather was a student at Vassar College in upstate New York, which is an area with lots of Lyme disease. She also comes from a part of New Jersey where the disease is widespread. So she might have picked up the disease while at college or during a visit home. Normally she is spunky and outgoing, so she was surprised to find herself feeling draggy, depressed, and achy. On a visit home, her mother suggested that she might have Lyme disease and took her to the doctor, who did blood tests. In all, she was tested for lupus, juvenile arthritis, mononucleosis, and Lyme disease. All of the tests came back negative. The doctor was not sure what she had and sent her home to get plenty of rest. As time went on, though, her joint pain got worse and she was feeling more and more fatigued.[2]

When she went to a different doctor, the Lyme disease blood test still came back negative. Because Heather's joints were so achy, she was tired all the time, and she lived in areas high in Lyme disease, the doctor decided she may have had the infection for the past two months. Since she had an early case, her doctor prescribed oral amoxicillin.[3]

A few days later, Heather became very frightened because her symptoms had gotten much worse. Her hip joints were so sore she could barely walk. Also, her hands had become swollen and sore, and she was passing out periodically. She wondered if she were about to die. Her doctor calmed her down, though. As she learned, she was having a typical reaction. Some Lyme disease patients actually get much worse

Even Governors Can Get Lyme Disease

Christine Todd Whitman is the governor of New Jersey. She has danced with television talk-show host David Letterman, she has filled in for Larry King on his radio show, and she has spoken at the Republican National Convention. She is an avid outdoorswoman who enjoys hiking and riding both horses and mountain bikes on forest trails. She is also one of the most famous people to have Lyme disease.[4]

The symptom she noticed most was being terribly fatigued all the time. At a press conference, she jokingly said she might have been feeling tired because she just turned fifty years old. She did take her Lyme disease seriously, however, and took the prescribed antibiotic, doxycycline.

It is probably no coincidence that Oldwick, where she makes her home, is in an area of New Jersey with one of the highest rates of Lyme disease. Her husband, John, came down with a telltale bull's-eye-shaped rash about the same time as she did. He was also treated for Lyme disease.

New Jersey governor Christine Todd Whitman contracted Lyme disease.

once they begin antibiotic treatment.[5] Heather continued taking her medicine and slowly got better. It was many months, however, before she really got all of her energy back. This too is not unusual. Medical researchers have found that many patients continue to feel tired even after antibiotic treatment. This fatigue can go on for months or even years.[6] Nobody really knows why this happens, but research is under way to find the cause.

How Antibiotics Work

Two common antibiotics used against the Lyme disease bacteria are amoxicillin and doxycycline. Amoxicillin is a chemically altered form of penicillin, which is a natural substance produced by bread mold. Amoxicillin kills bacteria by stopping them from making cell walls. Your body's cells do not have cell walls, but bacteria do. This is because bacteria live in a lot of different environments—the air, water, dirt, and in your body—and need a tough outer covering. Think of a bacterium's cell wall as being like a rugged off-road tire. It protects the delicate cell membrane—think of that as an inner tube—from being punctured as the bacterium bounces around from one place to another.

Amoxicillin stops certain strains of bacteria from assembling a tough cell wall. It is like taking a tire that is full of holes out for a drive. The first bump it hits—*ka-boom!*—there goes the inner tube. Without a protective cell wall, a bacterium would literally blow out.

Amoxicillin is an inexpensive antibiotic that is taken three to four times a day. Not everyone can take amoxicillin, because some people are allergic to it. That is why doctors often use another antibiotic, called doxycycline, to treat Lyme disease.

Doxycycline has to be taken only twice a day. This antibiotic works differently from amoxicillin. Doxycycline stops bacteria from making proteins. Without proteins, the bacteria cannot make or use energy. Instead of blowing up, they just fizzle out. One big advantage to using doxycycline is that it works against other diseases that ticks can carry, such as Rocky Mountain spotted fever or human granulocytic ehrlichiosis (HGE). Sometimes people can be infected with more than one kind of bacteria at a time, or a doctor might incorrectly believe that a person has Lyme disease bacteria when actually they have another kind of bacteria. In these cases, doxycycline will also kill the other bacteria.

There are other, more powerful, antibiotics such as one called ceftriaxone, which doctors can use when the bacteria have entered the brain. The trouble with some of these other antibiotics is that they cannot be given by mouth. Instead, they have to be given intravenously, that is, dripped slowly into the bloodstream through a needle inserted into a vein. This is a less comfortable and more expensive way of treating Lyme disease. Here we see another reason that it is important to be aware of the symptoms of Lyme disease and to catch it early.

6

Overdiagnosis and Chronic Lyme

There is no question that Lyme disease is a serious condition. If it is not caught and treated early, it can cause people to develop chronic fatigue, a feeling of constantly being tired. They might also develop joint pains and even memory problems. Even if it is caught late, the disease can still be cured with antibiotics. Before scientists discovered what was causing the disease, many people did not receive the necessary treatment and suffered needlessly for years. Once the *Borrelia burgdorferi* bacterium was discovered, federal and state health officials launched a campaign to educate the public about the dangers of tick bites.

Is Lyme Disease Overdiagnosed?

People living in areas where the Lyme disease bacteria are commonly found are now very aware of the risks of the disease. It is important for people to be on the lookout for Lyme disease, particularly during the summer and late fall and take precautions against tick bites. However, many medical researchers believe that the public, and even doctors, have gotten a bit too excited about Lyme disease.[1] They think that the public is trying to blame it for all kinds of symptoms that are actually being caused by other diseases. Some doctors have even been caught up in the trend to blame Lyme disease for a whole range of illnesses. In fact, studies show that about half of the people whose symptoms failed to clear up after they took antibiotics, never actually had the disease. It appears that too much of a good thing—that is, public awareness of Lyme disease—is not necessarily good. Some medical experts say that in certain parts of the country where Lyme disease is common, people have become hysterical about it.[2]

In one extreme case, dozens of children in New Jersey were hospitalized by a doctor who became convinced they all had Lyme disease.[3] Experts from the Centers for Disease Control (CDC), a federal laboratory that tracks down infectious diseases, became aware of the problem when they found that many children in the area were not attending school. So many children out of school must surely be a sign of an epidemic. When the CDC experts paid a visit to the area, they found that several children were not attending school because they were getting months-long treatments with a powerful intravenous antibiotic called ceftriaxone. This antibiotic can be toxic, especially to the gallbladder. In all, there were fourteen children who had to have their gallbladders removed, while many others got bloodstream infections as a result of their long-term antibiotic treatment. When the CDC experts checked into all the cases of Lyme disease diagnosed by the doctor, they found that only about 2 to 3 percent actually had Lyme disease.

One of the main reasons Lyme disease is overdiagnosed is that, other than the bull's-eye rash, the typical symptoms of Lyme disease are vague. After all, a lot of diseases can cause headaches, fever, and muscle or joint pains. On top of that, the tests for Lyme disease are not always reliable. Until better tests are developed, researchers expect that the overdiagnosis of Lyme disease will continue to be a problem.[4]

Chronic Lyme Disease

It is clear that too many people are being diagnosed with Lyme disease when they do not have it. But there is another important issue. About 10 percent of the patients who are *correctly* diagnosed with Lyme disease do not get well right away, even after faithfully taking the standard antibiotic treatment.[5] For months and sometimes years, they continue to have tremendous problems with fatigue, headaches, and memory loss. This long-term condition is now being called post-Lyme disease syndrome (PLDS). One of the unsolved mysteries about PLDS is whether this illness is caused by bacteria that hide in the brain and other parts of the body, thus avoiding a toxic dose of antibiotics.

Take the case of Vicki Logan, a woman from Westchester County, New York.[6] For four years she had headaches, fever, chronic fatigue, paralysis, and memory loss, all of which she

Because deer ticks live in the grass, small children are especially vulnerable to Lyme disease.

thought might be caused by Lyme disease. Her doctors did not believe she could possibly have it, though, because she had had the normal doses of antibiotics and she tested negative for the disease. Then she switched to a new doctor, who agreed she might have a lingering case of Lyme disease. When he gave her antibiotics, she seemed to get much better, but whenever he stopped them she got sick again.

When her doctor consulted Lyme disease experts at the Mayo Clinic in Rochester, Minnesota, they did not believe she actually had a chronic case of the disease. First of all, they doubted she ever had Lyme disease in the first place, and even if she did have it, all those antibiotics should have wiped it out. Still, Logan continued to be sick. Her doctor decided to take a sample of the fluid in her brain, called the cerebrospinal fluid. He sent it off to be tested by experts at the CDC. Sure enough, the CDC researchers found live bacteria swimming in the fluid and identified them as *Borrelia burgdorferi,* the Lyme disease bacteria. Logan and her doctor were vindicated, and she has made a slow recovery with intravenous antibiotics.

Cases like Logan's, in which people do not get rid of the bacteria despite repeated treatments with antibiotics, are thought to be pretty rare. Doctors do not fully understand why some patients stay sick for so long after getting Lyme disease.

Lyme disease expert Dr. John Halperin says that cases like Logan's are unusual. "I think persistent infection occurs, but it is very, very rare. There are a lot of people being labeled chronic Lyme [disease] with very little evidence of it. They

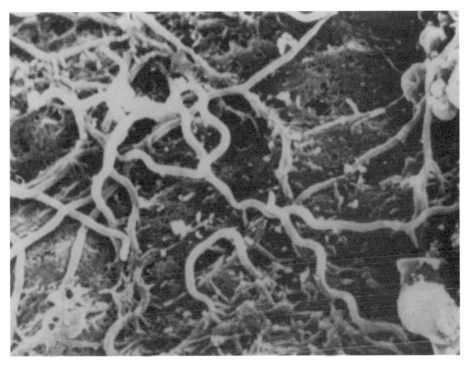

This is an electron microscope picture of *Borrelia burgdorferi,* the bacteria that cause Lyme disease.

don't have Lyme and so they won't respond to a zillion months of antibiotics."[7] He and other experts believe that some of the complaints of chronic Lyme disease are caused by tissue damage that occurred before the patients received antibiotics.[8]

Autoimmune disease is another possibility. What happens in autoimmune disease is that the patients' own immune system has turned against them after they got infected with bacteria or viruses. Here is how it works: On the surface of bacteria and viruses are proteins. Some of these proteins might look like a protein found naturally in the human body. In this case, the immune system will make antibodies that attack not just the protein on the bacteria, but also the body's own proteins. Even after the infection is over, the immune system will sometimes continue attacking normal, healthy tissues, causing serious autoimmune disease. This is thought to be the cause of multiple sclerosis, for instance, and it may be what is happening in people with post-Lyme disease syndrome.[9]

Still another possibility is that some of these people never really had Lyme disease at all. Instead, they may have another disease. The most common diseases that mimic some of the symptoms of Lyme disease are chronic fatigue syndrome and fibromyalgia. Chronic fatigue syndrome is a disease in which patients feel tired all the time from an unknown cause. Fibromyalgia is a condition in which patients feel aches and pains all over their bodies but do not actually have muscle or joint swelling or damage. The causes of chronic fatigue syndrome and fibromyalgia are not known.

Reasons That Lyme Disease Symptoms Might Linger

- Incorrect diagnosis—actually another disease
- Permanent tissue damage from Lyme disease
- Resistant infection with live *Borrelia burgdorferi* bacteria
- Dead *Borrelia burgdorferi* bacteria causing symptoms
- Autoimmune disease touched off by Lyme disease

7

Preventing Lyme Disease

In late May, tiny deer ticks, called nymphs, emerge from the ground. It is this event that kicks off the Lyme disease season each year. The season runs from about Memorial Day to Labor Day, and just about anyone who lives or works in a grassy or wooded area where Lyme disease is prevalent runs the risk of getting it. Lyme disease can be treated with antibiotics, but the best thing to do is to keep from getting it in the first place.

Where Lyme Disease Is Found

To prevent Lyme disease, you first need to know where it is usually found. If you live on a ranch in Montana, or in Los Angeles, Phoenix, or Austin, you have little to worry about. You have almost no chance of catching Lyme disease. To get it, you have to live in or visit an area of the country that is full of ticks that carry the Lyme disease bacteria.

People who have been diagnosed with Lyme disease can be found in almost every state in America. However, about 85 percent of all cases occur within about fifty miles of the coastal areas of Connecticut, Rhode Island, Massachusetts, New York, Pennsylvania, New Jersey, and Maryland. There is also a pocket of Lyme disease in eastern Minnesota and western Wisconsin. Plus, there is a bit of a problem in northern California and southern Oregon. Outside of these places, the risk of getting the disease is very low.

Lyme disease is not just a problem in this country. It is also found in Canada, Russia, northern China, Japan, and in many European countries, including Germany, Switzerland, Austria, and Sweden.[1]

Although most people who get Lyme disease live in rural and suburban areas, rats and mice that are infected with the Lyme disease bacteria have even been found in urban parks in big European cities like London, England, and Prague, Czech Republic. They have also been found in city parks in Bridgeport, Connecticut, and Baltimore, Maryland. So far, it is rare for a person to catch Lyme disease from the bite of a park-dwelling tick, but it sure is a possibility.[2]

The place where Lyme disease is most common is at the edge of heavily forested areas. New homes are often built where an area of forest has been cleared. A whole housing sub-division might be surrounded by forests. In these cases, it is not unusual to see deer strolling through the neighborhood.

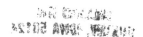

Although pretty, these deer drop ticks as they go. This is how people can get Lyme disease even if they never set foot in the deep woods. In one study of people bitten by ticks in Westchester County, New York, about 69 percent of them got a tick bite right in their own backyard. Because most people get Lyme disease right at home, this is the first place to think about getting rid of ticks.[3]

Personal Protection

There are plenty of things you can do to protect yourself against Lyme disease. The first step is to avoid the places where you are most likely to find ticks. Ticks are found mostly

States with the Highest Number of Lyme Disease Cases, 1996[4]

State	Number of Cases
New York	5,301
Connecticut	3,104
Pennsylvania	2,814
New Jersey	2,190
Rhode Island	534
Maryland	447
Wisconsin	396
Massachusetts	321
Minnesota	251
Delaware	173

on the leaves of tall grass and low shrubby vegetation. They do not fly or jump, and they do not drop down on people from trees. When a person or animal brushes against the plants, the tick crawls onto them.

If you do venture into tick habitat, you should wear light-colored clothing, which makes it easier to see a crawling tick. You should wear long pants and a long-sleeved shirt if you are going into the woods, or even into the backyard to play. Your pants should be tucked into the top of your socks or into boots to make it harder for the ticks to get to your skin.

Obviously, it is not easy to wear long-sleeved shirts and pants in the steamy heat of summertime. So if you are going outside in just shorts and a T-shirt, be sure to put on an insect repellent containing a high amount of DEET, a chemical that many insects avoid. Some companies even put out repellents that are specially formulated for use against ticks. Most of these repellents have the added bonus of keeping mosquitoes and flies away. Insect repellents should be used with caution, though. Keep the spray away from your mouth, eyes, open cuts, and sunburned skin. The chemicals in insect repellents can sometimes cause skin irritation. If this happens, you should wash the sore area with soap and water.

Permethrin is another chemical you can use; ticks especially dislike it. The U.S. Army uses this chemical to protect its soldiers from biting insects. Unfortunately, permethrin loses its potency if it is put directly onto the skin. It should be sprayed onto clothes and allowed to dry before you put them on. Use permethrin only with adult supervision.

This boy is wearing long-sleeved, light-colored clothing and is tucking his pants into his socks to avoid getting deer ticks on his skin.

Checking yourself for ticks should become a daily routine if you live in an area where Lyme disease is common. Because it is hard for you to look at every part of your body where a tick might be lurking, use the buddy system. Have a parent or a brother or sister look you over. Then you can return the favor. Why is it important to check for ticks every day? Scientists have learned that if a tick is removed within two days of first attaching itself, you probably will not get Lyme disease. It usually takes that long for the bacteria to make their way from the tick's gut to your skin.

Tick repellents will help keep deer ticks away.

Because the nymph lives close to the ground, carefully check your feet and legs. The ticks are hard to spot, so look carefully. Other prime places for ticks to dig in are the arms, neck, head, waist, and armpits. If you find one, follow the advice below.

Removing Ticks

Chances are that if you do look carefully for ticks, you may never see one even if it has bitten you. Only about 15 percent of ticks are discovered before they drink their fill of blood and drop off of a person's skin. The reason so few are found is that the most common form of biting tick is the tiny nymph. The nymphs cause about 90 percent of Lyme disease cases.

If you do find a tick, what should you do? The first thing is to show it to a parent or a doctor. The next step is critical. Some people think the best way to remove a tick is to light a match, blow it out, and touch the hot tip of the match to the back of the tick. The idea is that it will pull its head out of your skin. This usually does not work. The best way to remove the tick is to grab it with tweezers as close to the skin as possible and gently pull it free. There may be some of the tick's mouth parts left behind, but this is not a big problem. Simply wash the spot and then apply an antibiotic ointment.

After removing a tick, many people wonder if they should take an antibiotic, just in case the tick did carry the Lyme disease bacteria. It is not necessary to take an antibiotic right after being bitten, because only about one of every thirty people who remove a deer tick from their skin will actually develop Lyme disease.[5] Considering the cost

It is important to check the whole body, including the scalp, for ticks or for a rash.

and possible allergic reaction or side effects of taking antibiotics, medical experts say it is better to wait and see if a red spot or rash develops at the place where you were bitten, or if headaches and fever follow a week or two afterward. Then antibiotics can be taken to kill the bacteria.

Controlling Deer and Deer Ticks

Deer ticks can be killed with a number of insecticides. The best ones are carbaryl, Diazinon™, chlorpyrifos, and cyfluthrin.[6] Liquid insecticides can be sprayed onto the

74

Steps to Take to Avoid Lyme Disease[7]

Avoid grassy meadows and the edges of forests, especially during the peak tick season from May through July.

Wear light-colored clothing, including long sleeves and pants, because ticks will be easier to see against a light background.

Tuck pants into socks or boots to keep the ticks from reaching your skin.

Avoid sandals and other shoes that will easily let deer ticks get to your feet.

Use a tick repellent containing DEET on exposed skin (but not face and hands) and permethrin on clothing.

Check your body daily—including your hair—for ticks. Also check your pets for ticks.

If you find a tick, remove it promptly by grasping it with tweezers as close to the skin as possible. The risk of getting Lyme disease from a tick that is infected with the bacteria is much lower if it is removed within two days of first biting you.

lawn and vegetation. The trouble is that insecticides are poisonous. When they are sprayed onto the grass and shrubs, they can rub onto the skin. The best way to kill ticks is to spread the insecticides in the form of solid pellets, called granules. Although some of the granules land on grass or shrubs, most end up bouncing or dropping onto the ground. Tick larvae spend the winter in the soil. When they emerge as nymphs and encounter a granule of insecticide, they die.

It is critical to apply the insecticide at the right time. Experts recommend applying the granules to the lawn and other parts of the yard in about mid-May, which is when the nymph form of the deer tick first appears. Studies show that this use of insecticide can protect people from as many as 97 percent of the tick nymphs they might otherwise encounter.[8] A second application of pesticide might be needed in September to control the adult ticks.

Since it is mostly deer that carry deer ticks into contact with people, it would seem natural to simply keep deer away from people. This strategy can be very effective. Studies have shown that putting up a fence to keep deer out of an area reduces the number of deer tick nymphs by 80 percent.[9] The problem is that the fences have to be permanent. Plus, deer can jump, so the fences must be at least eight feet tall. Fences shorter than eight feet have to be electrified to work. For most people, such a fence is too expensive.

Some other ways to keep ticks away are to clear out all

the shrubby vegetation in the woods around the home. Simply chopping down the brush is not enough. It should be hauled away or burned. Otherwise, mice, which also carry ticks and the Lyme disease bacteria, will take up residence. For the same reasons, keep woodpiles away from the home. You should also consider planting shrubs that deer do not like and removing bird feeders, since they attract mice into the yard.

8

Future Directions

Lyme disease, first identified in America in the 1970s, can usually be cured by taking antibiotics for two to four weeks. Still, there is plenty of work ahead before the disease is considered under control. First, there is an intense effort under way to develop better diagnostic tests. With better tests, doctors will be able to tell with more certainty who has Lyme disease and who has some other disease that resembles Lyme disease. Researchers are also making a major effort toward creating a vaccine that will protect people from getting Lyme disease even if they are bitten by an infected tick. In fact, two vaccines have been submitted for approval to the Food and Drug Administration for use in preventing Lyme disease. Another study is looking at people with post-Lyme disease syndrome (PLDS).

Better Tests

As we saw in earlier chapters, many people are being tested and diagnosed with Lyme disease when they actually have some other problem. The tests for Lyme disease are not very reliable for several reasons. First of all, it is difficult to grow the Lyme disease bacteria, *Borrelia burgdorferi*, in a petri dish. Doctors grow bacteria on a petri dish to identify the type of bacteria causing an illness. Then the doctor can diagnose the illness correctly in order to treat it. For instance, when you have a sore throat, the doctor may suspect that you have strep throat, which is caused by an infection of streptococcus bacteria. To check for strep throat, the doctor will rub a swab deep inside your throat to capture some of the bacteria. The swab is then rubbed onto a petri dish. If there are streptococcus bacteria on the swab, they will grow on the dish and can be seen under a microscope. But it is not so simple with Lyme disease bacteria.

To check for Lyme disease, doctors have to test a patient's blood for antibodies, which are proteins the body uses to fight infection. The trouble is that the antibodies that are created to fight *Borrelia burgdorferi* can take up to eight weeks to develop. So most people who see their doctor for early symptoms, like a rash or fever and chills, do not have many of the antibodies in their blood. These people almost always test negative for Lyme disease. To cope with this problem, medical researchers are working on improved tests that do not depend on the body's antibodies.

One new test, called the antigen detection test, actually

puts a bit of the human immune system into a test tube.[1] This test uses white blood cells that have been extracted from the blood of people who previously had Lyme disease. The extracted cells are then grown in large numbers to create an "army" of white blood cells ready for action against *Borrelia burgdorferi*. When they are mixed with blood or some other fluid from a person who is thought to have Lyme disease, they swarm around, hunting for the bacteria. If they find what they are looking for—that is, live bacteria or bits of protein from it—they swing into action and begin multiplying. Pretty soon, a large increase in the number of white blood cells can be seen under the microscope. This increase signifies that the patient's blood is infected with the bacteria that cause Lyme disease.

Another test being developed is called PCR, which stands for polymerase chain reaction. With the PCR test, the doctor is looking for DNA from *Borrelia burgdorferi*. What makes this test so valuable is that it can detect even the tiniest amount of bacterial DNA in a patient's blood, whether the bacteria are live or dead. In the PCR test, a patient's blood sample is mixed with an enzyme called taq polymerase. This enzyme is found in most living cells, where its job is to make exact copies of DNA. In this test, taq polymerase copies the bacterial DNA over and over again, until as many as a million are made. Try doing that with a photocopier! Now that there is plenty of the bacterial DNA in the sample, the person doing the test can add pieces of DNA, called probes, that will stick to the bacterial DNA. Attached to the probes are molecules that glow when exposed to ultraviolet light. Now it is easy to see whether the patient's blood sample contains DNA from *Borrelia burgdorferi*.

Armed with these tests, doctors will not have to depend so much on symptoms to know if someone has Lyme disease. The new tests should make it easier to detect Lyme disease in its early stages and to weed out those people who have been falsely diagnosed with the disease.

Vaccines

A vaccine against Lyme disease would make life a lot simpler for people living where the disease is prevalent. The trouble is that the only Lyme disease vaccine that has been available is for animals. The animal vaccine is very simple. It is made from whole *Borrelia burgdorferi* bacteria that have been killed. This approach is not considered safe enough for people, though. Bacteria contain all sorts of proteins, and each protein has the potential for causing an allergic reaction.

A better approach is to make a vaccine from just one of the proteins found on the surface of the bacteria. Vaccines like this have been tested by two drug companies.[2] The companies have taken a single protein, called outer-surface protein A (OspA), and injected it into human volunteers. The body then forms antibodies to this protein. If *Borrelia burgdorferi* bacteria try to infect the body, the antibodies are ready to attack and wipe them out. In September 1997, both companies announced good results when they tried out their vaccines on people under age sixty. One vaccine, made by SmithKline Beecham of Philadelphia, stopped 90 percent of the cases of Lyme disease that would otherwise have been expected to develop. The other vaccine, from Pasteur Merieux Connaught of Swiftwater, Pennsylvania, was even better, preventing Lyme disease almost 100 percent of the time. The only side effect seems to be pain at the point of injection.[3] Now it is up to the Food and Drug Administration (FDA) to decide if the vaccines are safe and effective enough to use in people.

Some companies plan to start testing other vaccine possibilities. One of the companies, MedImmune, Inc., is thinking of switching its focus to a different protein, called DBP, which remains in the same form in all the Lyme disease bacteria.

No vaccine provides 100 percent protection against disease, however. So even if a Lyme disease vaccine is approved by the FDA, precautions against ticks will still be necessary.

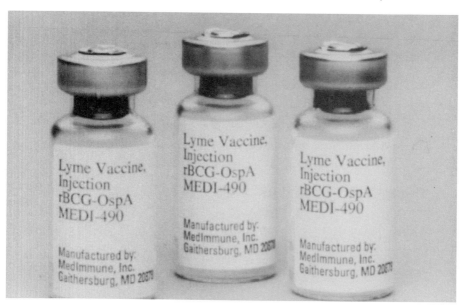

A Lyme disease vaccine is under development.

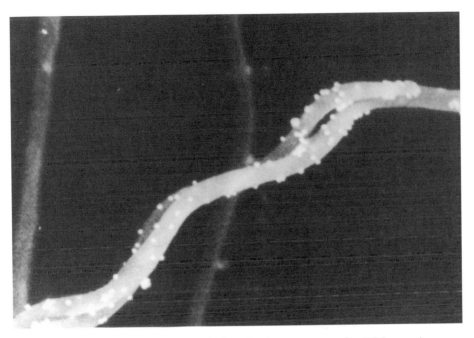

In a close-up view of *B. burgdorferi*, the dots represent the DBP protein that is found all over the surface.

Research on Post-Lyme Disease Syndrome

Lyme disease researchers are also looking at what is causing the lingering symptoms called post-Lyme disease syndrome (PLDS). PLDS is a condition in which people's Lyme disease symptoms take months or years to go away, instead of the usual few weeks. Scientists think that in some of these people the bacteria may dodge the immune system by hiding inside the body's cells.[4]

The National Institutes of Health began a $4-million study of PLDS in the summer of 1996. In this study, scientists

83

will try to find out which tests are best for determining if someone is really infected with the Lyme disease bacteria. They will also test several kinds of antibiotics for treating the disease. It will be several years before the results of the study are known.

Lyme disease is a serious illness, but it has received serious attention. As a result, the future looks bright for people in regions where the disease is prevalent. Ways of keeping deer ticks and people from coming in contact with each other have been developed. Better tests will soon make diagnosis more precise, so that the disease can be caught and cured early. Also, vaccinations should be available sometime soon. In the very near future, Lyme disease should be a far less serious threat than it is today.

Q & A

Q. Where did Lyme disease get its name?

A. Lyme disease got its name from the town of Old Lyme, Connecticut, the place where the disease was first identified in this country in the 1970s.

Q. What kind of bacteria causes Lyme disease?

A. The bacteria are called spirochetes because of their spiral shape. The scientific name is *Borrelia burgdorferi*, in honor of the discoverer, Willy Burgdorfer.

Q. During the summer I found a small tick embedded in the skin on my leg, and I pulled it off. Does this mean I have Lyme disease? Should I take antibiotics?

A. Probably not. The chance of any one tick bite causing Lyme disease is low. The best thing to do after gently removing a tick with tweezers is to watch that spot. If a red rash appears or if you get a flulike illness, headaches, or joint pains, see your doctor right away.

Q. One of my classmates was just treated for Lyme disease. Can I catch it from her? Should I be tested too?

A. The bacteria that cause Lyme disease are spread only by the bite of a deer tick. So there is no cause for alarm if you come in contact with another person who has the disease.

Q. Why is Lyme disease so much in the news these days?

A. Prior to the 1970s, there were few Lyme disease cases reported. But as more trees have grown back in the Northeast and other parts of the country, and as populations of white-tailed deer have risen dramatically, Lyme disease has become a much larger problem. There are simply far more deer ticks present today, and far more chances for people to come in contact with them.

Q. My uncle got Lyme disease and has been sick for the last three years. He has not even been able to go to work in all this time. What is wrong with him?

A. For the majority of people who catch Lyme disease, two to four weeks of antibiotics clears it up for good. But medical experts are still not sure what is happening in the small percentage of people, such as your uncle, who fail to get over Lyme disease quickly. Most researchers do not believe that these people are still infected with the bacteria especially if they have been properly treated with antibiotics. Instead, the extreme fatigue, headaches, and joint pains they have are called post-Lyme disease syndrome (PLDS). Research is under way to try to figure out why such people are not getting well quickly. Some researchers think these people are actually suffering from other diseases, such as chronic fatigue syndrome or fibromyalgia.

Q. Can my pets get Lyme disease?

A. Yes, they can, particularly dogs. There is now a vaccine that can help protect dogs against Lyme disease.

Lyme Disease Timeline

1909—Swedish dermatologist Dr. Arvid Afzelius first describes a bull's-eye rash in a patient.

1913—Austrian Dr. B. Lipschütz notices that the rashes last a long time, and calls them erythema chronicum migrans (ECM).

1922—French doctors report seeing patients who are paralyzed after being bitten by ticks.

1949—Swedish doctor Sven Hellerström first reports that meningitis often follows the ECM rash.

1955—Dr. H. Gotz and four other researchers inject themselves with the skin from a patient's ECM rash; they get the rash and cure it with penicillin.

1970—ECM rashes are seen for the first time in Wisconsin.

1972—ECM is reported in Connecticut.

1975—Major outbreak of children's arthritis was brought to the attention of authorities. Yale University researchers, led by Dr. Allen Steere, launch investigation.

1978—Yale researchers find that tick bites cause Lyme disease.

1981—Dr. Willy Burgdorfer finds spirochetes in ticks and links them to Lyme disease.

1982—Centers for Disease Control (CDC) begins keeping track of number of cases of Lyme disease. CDC finds fewer than five hundred people are infected.

1984—Lyme disease bacterium is named *Borrelia burgdorferi* in honor of Dr. Burgdorfer.

1996—National Institutes of Health begins a major research study of chronic Lyme disease; a record number of cases of Lyme disease—16,461—are reported to Centers for Disease Control.

1997—Clinical trials of Lyme disease vaccine are completed; vaccines submitted to Food and Drug Administration for approval.

For More Information

American Lyme Disease Foundation, Inc.
Mill Pond Offices
293 Route 100
Somers, NY 10589
(914) 277-6970
Fax: (914) 277-6974
Email: ALDF@computer.net
Website: http://www.w2.com/docs2/d5/lyme.html

Centers for Disease Control and Prevention (CDC)
Atlanta, GA 30333
(404) 639-3311
Voice and Fax Information: (888) 232-3228 (24 hours)
Website: http://www.cdc.gov/ncidod/diseases/lyme/lyme.htm

Lyme Disease Foundation
1 Financial Plaza, 18th Floor
Hartford, CT 06103-2601
(860) 525-2000
Fax: (860) 525-8425
Information Hotline: (800) 886-LYME (24 hours)
Website: http://www.lyme.org

National Institute of Allergy and Infectious Diseases
NIAID Chronic Lyme Disease Study
Building 10, Room 11N228
10 Center Drive, MSC 1888

Bethesda, MD 20892-1888
(800) 772-5464, ext. 605
Fax: (301) 496-7383
Website: http://www.niaid.nih.gov

In Canada:
Lyme Disease Association of Ontario
365 St. David Street South
Fergus, Ontario N1M 2L7
(519) 843-3646
Fax: (519) 843-6550

Vancouver, B.C., Lyme Borreliosis Society
P.O. Box 91535
West Vancouver, British Columbia V7V 3P2
(604) 922-3704

Selected State Health Departments
(for those areas with a high incidence of Lyme disease):
California Department of Health Services
Division of Communicable Disease Control
2151 Berkeley Way, Room 708
Berkeley, CA 94704
(510) 540-2566

Connecticut State Department of Public Health
Community Health
Infectious Disease Epidemiology
410 Capitol Ave.
Hartford, CT 06106
(860) 509-7994

Maryland Department of Health and Mental Hygiene
Epidemiology and Disease Control
201 West Preston St.
Baltimore, MD 21201
(410) 767-5441

Massachusetts Department of Public Health
State Laboratory Institute
Epidemiology Division
305 South St.
Jamaica Plain, MA 02130
(617) 983-6800

Minnesota Department of Health
Center for Disease Control
717 Delaware St. Southeast
Minneapolis, MN 55440
(612) 623-5363

New Jersey Department of Health
Infectious and Zoonotic Disease Program
P.O. Box 369
Trenton, NJ 08625-0369
(609) 588-7500

New York City Department of Health
Bureau of Communicable Disease
125 Worth St.
New York, NY 10013
(212) 788-4204

New York State Department of Health
Arthropod-Borne Disease Program
Empire State Plaza, Corning Tower, Room 621
Albany, NY 12237
(518) 474-4568

Oregon Health Division
Acute and Communicable Disease Program
800 Northeast Oregon St., Suite 772
Portland, OR 97232
(503) 731-4024

Pennsylvania State Department of Health
Division of Communicable Disease Epidemiology
P.O. Box 90
Harrisburg, PA 17108
(717) 787-3350

Rhode Island Department of Health
Office of Communicable Disease
3 Capitol Hill
Providence, RI 02908
(401) 277-2432

Wisconsin Department of Health and Family Services
Division of Health, Bureau of Public Health
1414 East Washington, Room 241
Madison, WI 53703
(608) 267-9003

Chapter Notes

Chapter 1. Three Lyme Disease Stories

1. Personal communication with Dr. Rosalynn Kerson, mother of Henry, Pleasantville, New York, December 14, 1996.

2. Marc Wortman, "Charge of the Lyme Brigade," *Yale Medicine: Alumni Bulletin of the School of Medicine*, vol. 30, May 15, 1996, p. 8.

3. Personal communication with L'anna Burton, mother of Jason, Groton, Connecticut, January 6, 1997.

4. Personal communication with Libby Grimm, mother of Norm, Sanibel Island, Florida, October 25, 1996.

Chapter 2. The Discovery of Lyme Disease

1. Edward D. Harris, Jr., "Lyme Disease Success for Academia and the Community," *New England Journal of Medicine*, vol. 308, March 31, 1983, pp. 773–774.

2. Polly Murray, *The Widening Circle: A Lyme Disease Pioneer Tells Her Story* (New York: St. Martin's Press, 1996), p. 13.

3. Ibid., p. 86.

4. Boyce Rensberger, "A New Type of Arthritis Found in Lyme," *New York Times*, July 18, 1976, p. A1, 39.

5. Willy Burgdorfer, "Discovery of *Borrelia burgdorferi*," in *Lyme Disease*, ed. Patricia K. Coyle (St. Louis: Mosby–Year Book, 1993), p. 5.

6. Personal communication with Dr. Willy Burgdorfer, Hamilton, Montana, November 23, 1996.

7. Ibid.

8. Ibid.

9. Centers for Disease Control (CDC), "Emerging Infectious Diseases: Lyme Disease—United States, 1991–1992," *Morbidity and Mortality Weekly Report (MMWR)*, vol. 42, May 14, 1993, pp. 345–348; and CDC, "Lyme Disease—United States, 1995," *MMWR*, vol. 45, June 14, 1996,

pp. 481–484. CDC, "Lyme Disease—United States, 1996," *MMWR*, vol. 46, June 13, 1997, pp. 531–535.

10. Personal communication with Dr. Willy Burgdorfer, Hamilton, Montana, November 23, 1996.

11. William F. Marshall III et al., "Detection of *Borrelia burgdorferi* DNA in Museum Specimens of *Peromyscus leucopus*," *Journal of Infectious Diseases*, vol. 170, October 1994, pp. 1027–1032.

12. Franz-Rainer Matuschka et al., "Antiquity of the Lyme-Disease Spirochaete in Europe," *Lancet*, vol. 346, November 18, 1995, p. 1367.

13. Personal communication with Terri McFadden, museum curator, Museum of Comparative Zoology, Cambridge, MA, September 15, 1997.

14. Andrew Spielman, "The Emergence of Lyme Disease and Human Babesiosis in a Changing Environment," *Annals of the New York Academy of Sciences,* vol. 740, December 15, 1994, pp. 150–153.

Chapter 3. What Is Lyme Disease?

1. Information on tick life cycle from Durland Fish, "Environmental Risk and Prevention of Lyme Disease," *American Journal of Medicine*, vol. 98 (suppl. 4A), April 24, 1995, pp. 4A-2S–4A-4S; and Alan G. Barbour, Lyme Disease: The Cause, the Cure, the Controversy (Baltimore: Johns Hopkins University Press, 1996), pp. 52–57.

2. James J. Nocton and Allen C. Steere, "Lyme Disease," *Advances in Internal Medicine*, vol. 40, 1995, p. 80.

3. Information on late stages of Lyme disease from ibid., pp. 83–86; Jorge L. Benach and James L. Coleman, "Overview of Spirochetal Infections," in *Lyme Disease*, ed. Patricia K. Coyle (St. Louis: Mosby–Year Book, 1993), p. 64; and American Lyme Disease Foundation, *Lyme Disease: Clinical Update for Physicians* (Somers, N.Y.: ALDF, 1993), pp. 4–5.

4. Donald B. Middleton, "Tick-Borne Infections," *Postgraduate Medicine*, vol. 95, April 1994, p. 131.

5. Peter J. Krause et al., "Concurrent Lyme Disease and Babesiosis: Evidence for Increased Severity and Duration of Illness," *Journal of the*

American Medical Association, vol. 275, no. 21, June 5, 1996, pp. 1657–1660.

6. Middleton, p. 132.

7. Daniel B. Fishbein and David T. Dennis, "Tick-Borne Diseases—A Growing Risk," *New England Journal of Medicine*, vol. 333, no. 7, August 17, 1995, pp. 452–453.

Chapter 4. Diagnosing Lyme Disease

1. Personal communication with John Green, New London, Connecticut, December 4, 1996.

2. Ibid.

3. Michael A. Gerber et al., "Lyme Disease in Children in Southeastern Connecticut," *New England Journal of Medicine*, vol. 335, no. 17, October 24, 1996, p. 1273.

4. Marc G. Golightly, "Antibody Assays," in *Lyme Disease*, ed. Patricia K. Coyle (St. Louis: Mosby–Year Book, 1993), p. 116, 118.

5. Gerber et al., p. 1271.

6. Bruce Alberts et al., *Molecular Biology of the Cell*, 3rd ed. (New York: Garland Publishing, 1994), pp. 1195-1254.

7. American Lyme Disease Foundation, *Lyme Disease: Clinical Update for Physicians* (Somers, N.Y.: ALDF, 1993), p. 6.

8. Henry M. Feder, Jr., and Margaret S. Hunt, "Pitfalls in the Diagnosis and Treatment of Lyme Disease in Children," *Journal of the American Medical Association*, vol. 274, no. 1, July 5, 1995, p. 66.

9. Ibid.

10. Ibid.

Chapter 5. Treating Lyme Disease

1. Personal communication with Jona Burton, interviewed with permission of her mother, L'anna Burton, Groton, Connecticut, January 6, 1997.

2. Personal communication with Heather Malin, New York City, New York, December 12, 1996.

3. Ibid.

4. Mary Jo Layton, "The Big 50—Whitman Celebrates Her Birthday Today," *The Record, Northern New Jersey*, September 26, 1996, p. A3.

5. Alan G. Barbour, M.D., *Lyme Disease: The Cause, the Cure, the Controversy* (Baltimore: Johns Hopkins University Press, 1996), p. 120.

6. Lauren B. Krupp et al., "Fatigue," in *Lyme Disease*, ed. Patricia K. Coyle (St. Louis: Mosby–Year Book, 1993), p. 199.

Chapter 6. Overdiagnosis and Chronic Lyme

1. Marc Wortman, "Getting Beyond the Fear of Lyme Disease," *Yale Medicine: Alumni Bulletin of the School of Medicine*, vol. 30, May 15, 1996, p. 9.

2. Mary Brewster, "Common Antibiotics Effective in Children's Lyme Disease," United Press International newswire, October 24, 1996.

3. Diana Jean Schemo, "Prolonged Lyme Treatments Posing Risks, Experts Warn," *New York Times*, January 4, 1994, pp. A1, B5.

4. Ibid.; and Eliot Marshall, "NIH Gears Up to Test a Hotly Disputed Theory," *Science*, October 13, 1995, pp. 228–229.

5. Information on chronic Lyme disease and PLDS is from Leonard H. Sigal, "Persisting Complaints Attributed to Chronic Lyme Disease," *American Journal of Medicine*, vol. 96, April 1994, pp. 365–374; and Alan G. Barbour and Durland Fish, "The Biological and Social Phenomenon of Lyme Disease," *Science*, vol. 260, June 11, 1993, pp. 1610–1616.

6. Elisabeth Rosenthal, "Lyme Disease: Does It Really Linger?" *New York Times*, August 24, 1993, p. C1.

7. Ibid.

8. Ibid.

9. National Institute of Allergy and Infectious Diseases, "Questions and Answers About NIAID's Chronic Lyme Disease Study," June 1996, p. 1.

Chapter 7. Preventing Lyme Disease

1. Andrew Spielman, "The Emergence of Lyme Disease and Human Babesiosis in a Changing Environment," *Annals of the New York Academy of Sciences*, vol. 740, December 15, 1994, p. 149; Johan Berglund et al., "An Epidemiologic Study of Lyme Disease in Southern Sweden," *New England Journal of Medicine*, vol. 333, November 16, 1995, pp. 1319–1324.

2. Franz-Rainer Matuschka, "Risk of Urban Lyme Disease Enhanced by the Presence of Rats," *Journal of Infectious Diseases*, vol. 174, November 1996, pp. 1108–1111.

3. Durland Fish, "Environmental Risk and Prevention of Lyme Disease," *American Journal of Medicine*, vol. 98 (suppl. 4A), April 24, 1995, p. 4A-5S.

4. Centers for Disease Control, "Lyme Disease—United States, 1996," *Morbidity and Mortality Weekly Report*, vol. 46, no. 23, June 13, 1997, p. 533.

5. James J. Nocton and Allen C. Steere, "Lyme Disease," *Advances in Internal Medicine*, vol. 40, 1995, p. 98.

6. Fish, p. 4A-5S.

7. Ibid.; and John Nowakowski and Gary P. Wormser, "Treatment of Early Lyme Disease: Infection Associated with Erythema Migrans," in *Lyme Disease*, ed. Patricia K. Coyle (St. Louis: Mosby–Year Book, 1993), p. 156.

8. Fish, p. 4A-5S.

9. Ibid., p. 4A-6S.

Chapter 8. Future Directions

1. Information on new tests from David Dorward, "Laboratory Diagnostic Tests for Lyme Disease," *LymeNet Newsletter*, March 10, 1993, pp. 1–12.

2. Personal communication with Mark Kaufmann, manager of strategic planning and investor relations, MedImmune, Inc., January 6, 1997.

3. Ridgely Ochs,"Results Are In on 2nd Lyme Vaccine," *Newsday*, September 17, 1997, p. A22.

4. Lauric K. Doepel, "Chronic Lyme Disease—Is It an Ongoing Infection?" *Dateline: NIAID*, June 1996, p. 7; and Eliot Marshall, "NIH Gears Up to Test a Hotly Disputed Theory," *Science*, vol. 270, October 13, 1995, pp. 228–229.

Glossary

antibiotics—Drugs that kill bacteria.

arthritis—Swelling of a joint, causing great pain.

autoimmune disease—A disease in which the immune system attacks the body's own tissues.

bacteria—Single-celled microscopic organisms that can sometimes cause infections. (The singular of "bacteria" is "bacterium.")

Bell's palsy—A drooping of the face caused by a paralyzed nerve.

Borrelia burgdorferi—Scientific name of the bacteria that cause Lyme disease.

chronic fatigue syndrome (CFS)—A condition in which a patient often feels tired but is not known to be sick with any disease.

deer tick—A tiny tick that can carry the bacteria that cause Lyme disease. The scientific name of the deer tick is *Ixodes scapularis.*

DEET (N,N-diethyl-meta-toluamide)—A chemical used as an insect repellent to ward off ticks and other insects.

DNA (deoxyribonucleic acid)—An extremely long molecule, found in the center of cells, which carries codes for all the proteins in the body.

erythema chronicum migrans (ECM)—The bull's-eye rash typical of Lyme disease.

fibromyalgia—A condition in which a patient feels aches and pains all over but does not actually have muscle or joint swelling or damage. The cause is unknown.

Food and Drug Administration (FDA)—The federal agency that decides which drugs are safe for humans.

genes—Made of DNA, a single gene tells a cell to make a certain protein. This protein then performs certain important functions.

insecticide—A chemical that kills insects.

insect repellent—A chemical that insects avoid.

larvae—The immature form of tick that hatches from the egg.

Lyme, Connecticut—The place in the United States where the first outbreaks of Lyme disease were found.

National Institutes of Health (NIH)—A U.S. government agency that conducts much of the research into human diseases. It also gives out grants to medical researchers across the country.

nymph—The one-year-old immature form of the deer tick. The nymph is responsible for most cases of Lyme disease.

permethrin—A potent insect repellent used only on clothing. It is also called Permanone and Duranon.

polymerase chain reaction (PCR)—A new and very sensitive type of test for Lyme disease.

post-Lyme disease syndrome (PLDS)—A mysterious, lingering illness that occasionally follows Lyme disease.

rash—A red, swollen area of the skin.

spirochetes—Spiral-shaped bacteria.

syndrome—A group of symptoms (such as a rash, fever, headache, etc.) that indicates the presence of a particular illness.

virus—A microscopic long string of genetic material enclosed in a protective protein shell. It cannot live outside a living organism, and must insert itself into other cells in order to reproduce itself.

Further Reading

Books

Barbour, Alan G., M.D. *Lyme Disease: The Cause, the Cure, the Controversy.* Baltimore: Johns Hopkins University Press, 1996.

Coyle, Patricia K., ed. *Lyme Disease.* St. Louis: Mosby–Year Book, 1993.

Murray, Polly. *The Widening Circle: A Lyme Disease Pioneer Tells Her Story.* New York: St. Martin's Press, 1996.

Articles

Altman, Lawrence K. "Possible Dual Threat from Ticks: Lyme and Another Disease, as Well." *New York Times,* June 11, 1996, p. C7.

Barbour, Alan G., and Durland Fish. "The Biological and Social Phenomenon of Lyme Disease." *Science,* vol. 260, June 11, 1993, pp. 1610–1616.

Brody, Jane E. "Frequent Overdiagnosis of Lyme Disease Found." *New York Times,* April 14, 1993, p. C12.

————. "Plight of Lyme Patients Lost in the Statistics." *New York Times,* August 25, 1993, p. C10.

————. "When Lyme Invades the Brain and Spinal System." *New York Times,* February 15, 1995, p. C8.

Centers for Disease Control, "Lyme Disease—United States, 1995." *Morbidity and Mortality Weekly Report,* vol. 45, June 14, 1996, pp. 481–484.

Feder, Henry M., Jr., and Margaret S. Hunt. "Pitfalls in the Diagnosis and Treatment of Lyme Disease in Children." *Journal of the American Medical Association*, vol. 274, no. 1, July 5, 1995, pp. 66–68.

Fishbein, Daniel B., and David T. Dennis. "Tick-Borne Diseases—A Growing Risk." *New England Journal of Medicine*, vol. 333, no. 7, August 17, 1995, pp. 452–453.

Gerber, Michael A., et. al. "Lyme Disease in Children in Southeastern Connecticut." *New England Journal of Medicine*, vol. 335, no. 17, October 24, 1996, pp. 1270–1274.

Harris, Edward D., M.D. "Lyme Disease—Success for Academia and the Community." *New England Journal of Medicine*, vol. 308, March 31, 1983, pp. 773–774.

Nocton, James J., and Steere, Allen C. "Lyme Disease." *Advances in Internal Medicine*, vol. 40, 1995, pp. 69–117

Rensberger, Boyce. "Matching Lyme Disease Bacteria's Diabolical Versatility." *Washington Post*, June 19, 1995, p. A3.

Rosenthal, Elisabeth. "Lyme Disease: Does It Really Linger?" *New York Times*, August 24, 1993, pp. C1, C8.

Schemo, Diana Jean. "Prolonged Lyme Treatments Posing Risks, Experts Warn." *New York Times*, January 4, 1994, pp. A1, B5.

Spielman, Andrew. "The Emergence of Lyme Disease and Human Babesiosis in a Changing Environment." *Annals of the New York Academy of Sciences*, vol. 740, December 15, 1994, pp. 146–156.

Weiss, Rick. "Lyme Disease Traced to Late 19th Century." *Washington Post*, November 22, 1994, Health section, p. 5.

Index